COLORING FOR CALMNESS

BY YOLANDA PIGATT

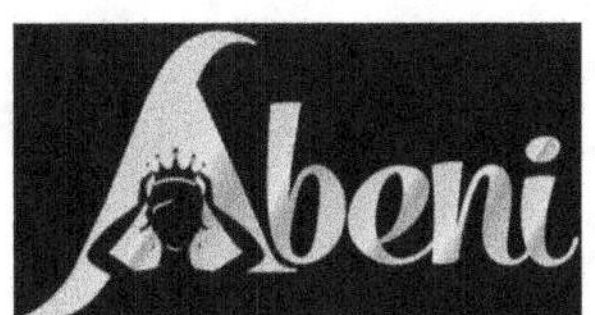

Copyright @ 2022 Abeni Publishing

ISBN: 979-8-9873862-0-0

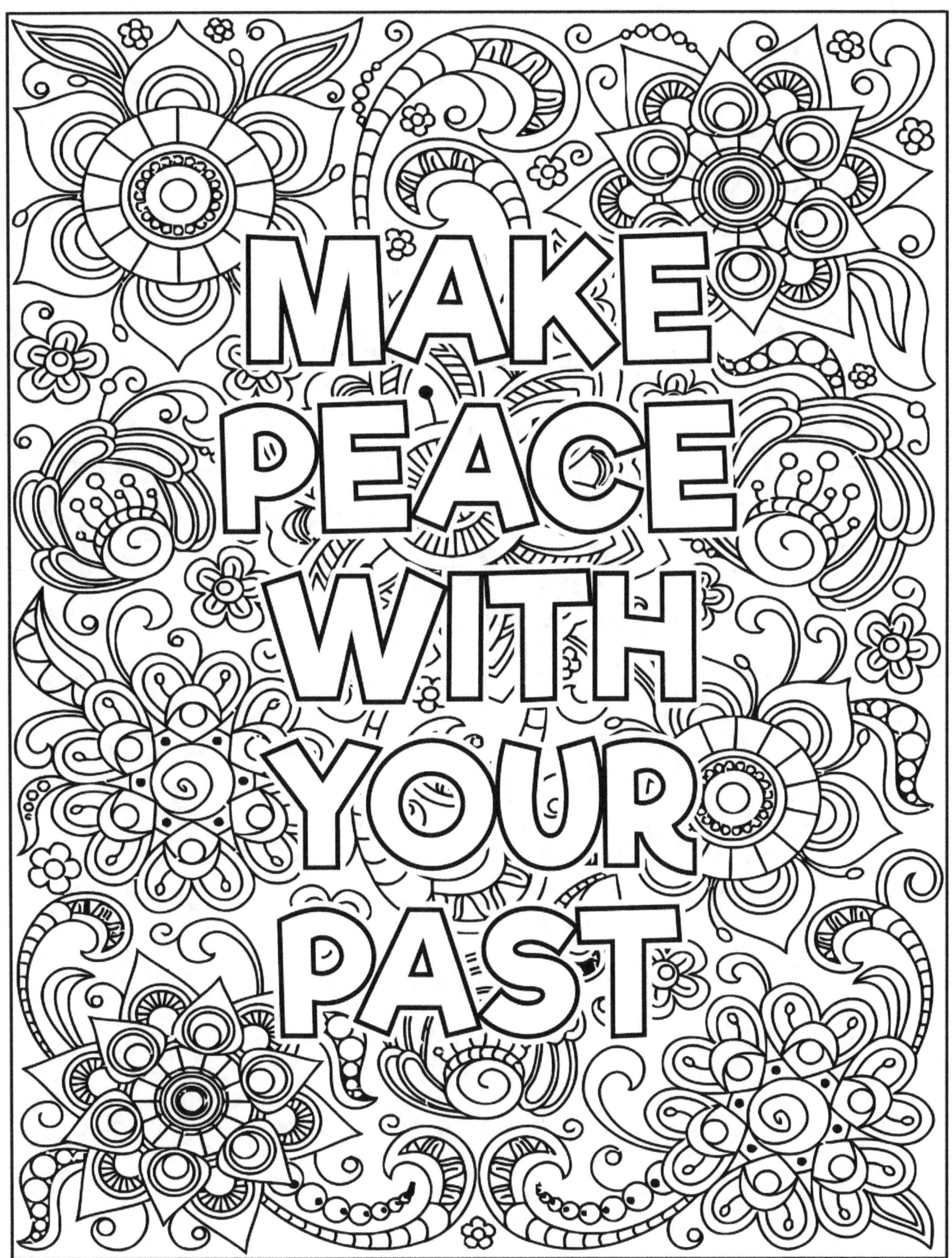

MAKE
PEACE
WITH
YOUR
PAST

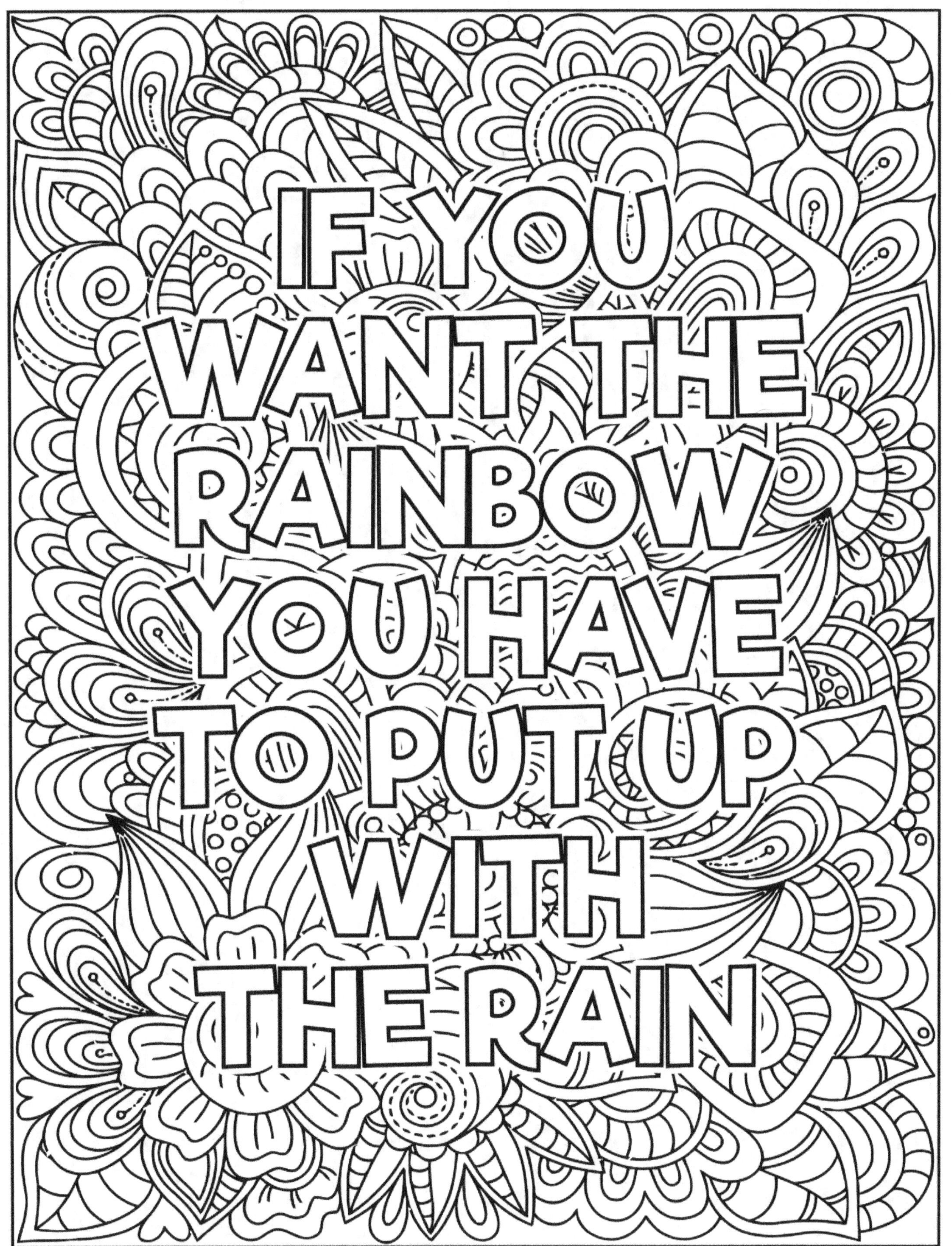

IF YOU WANT THE RAINBOW YOU HAVE TO PUT UP WITH THE RAIN

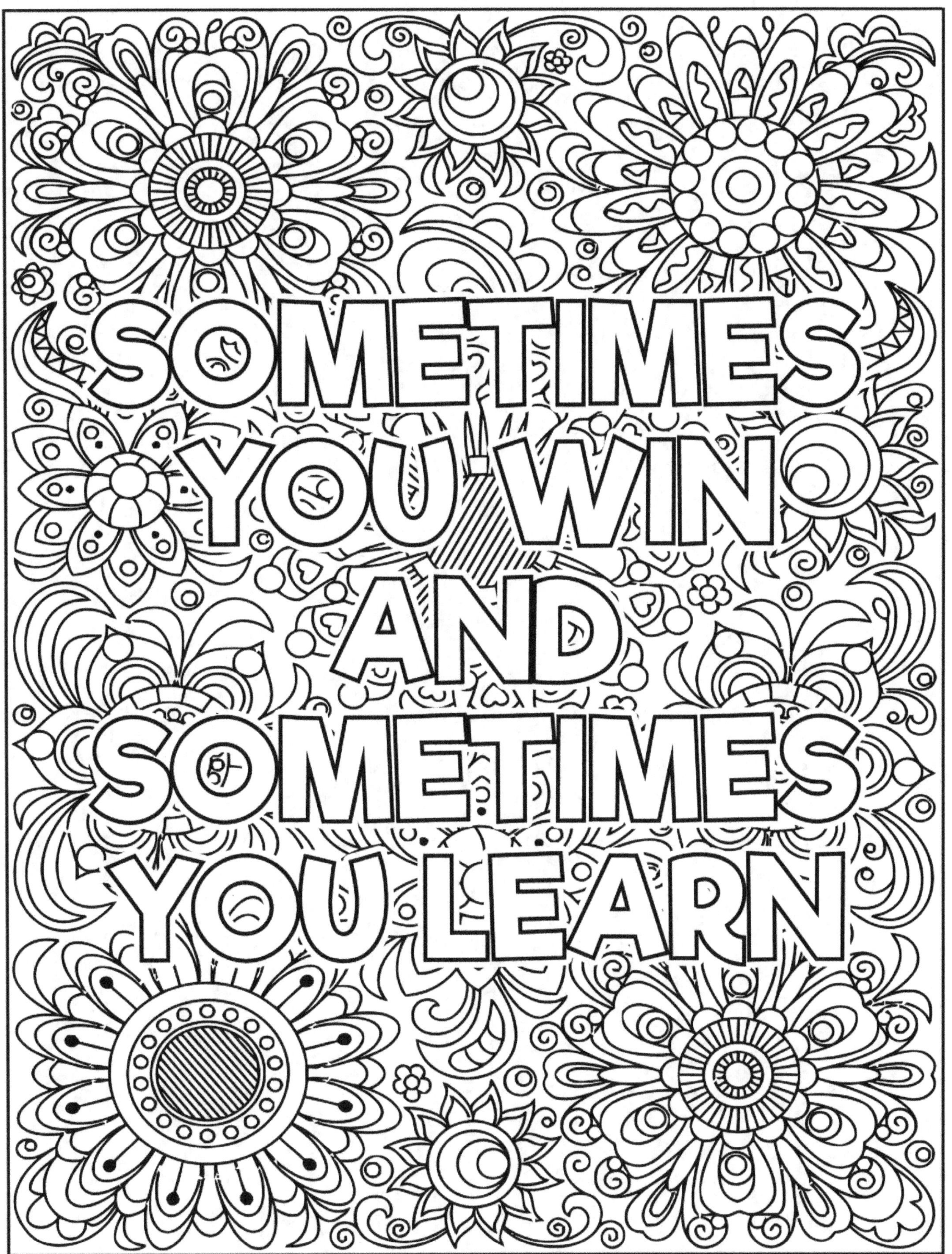

SOMETIMES YOU WIN AND SOMETIMES YOU LEARN

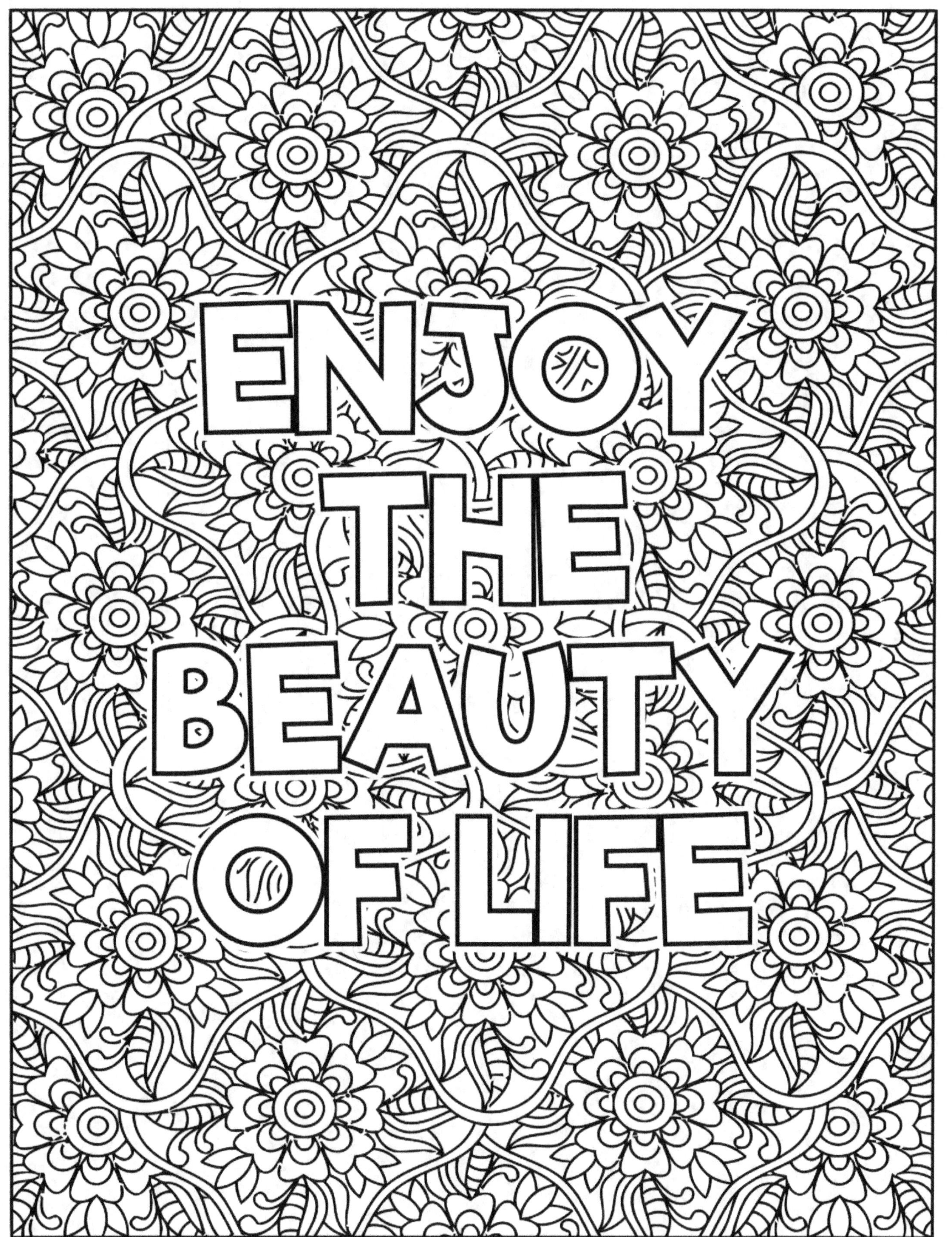

ENJOY
THE
BEAUTY
OF LIFE

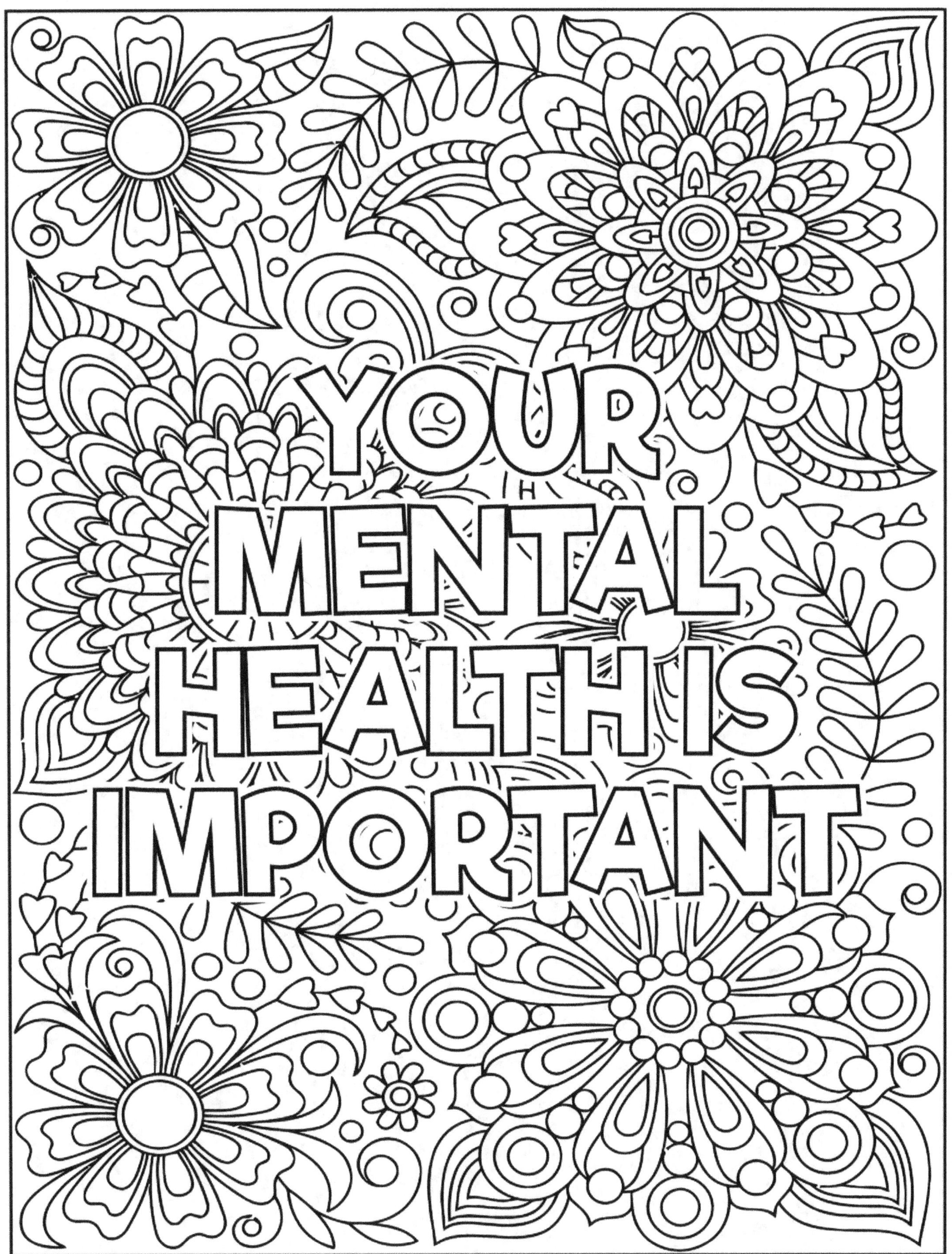

YOUR
MENTAL
HEALTH IS
IMPORTANT

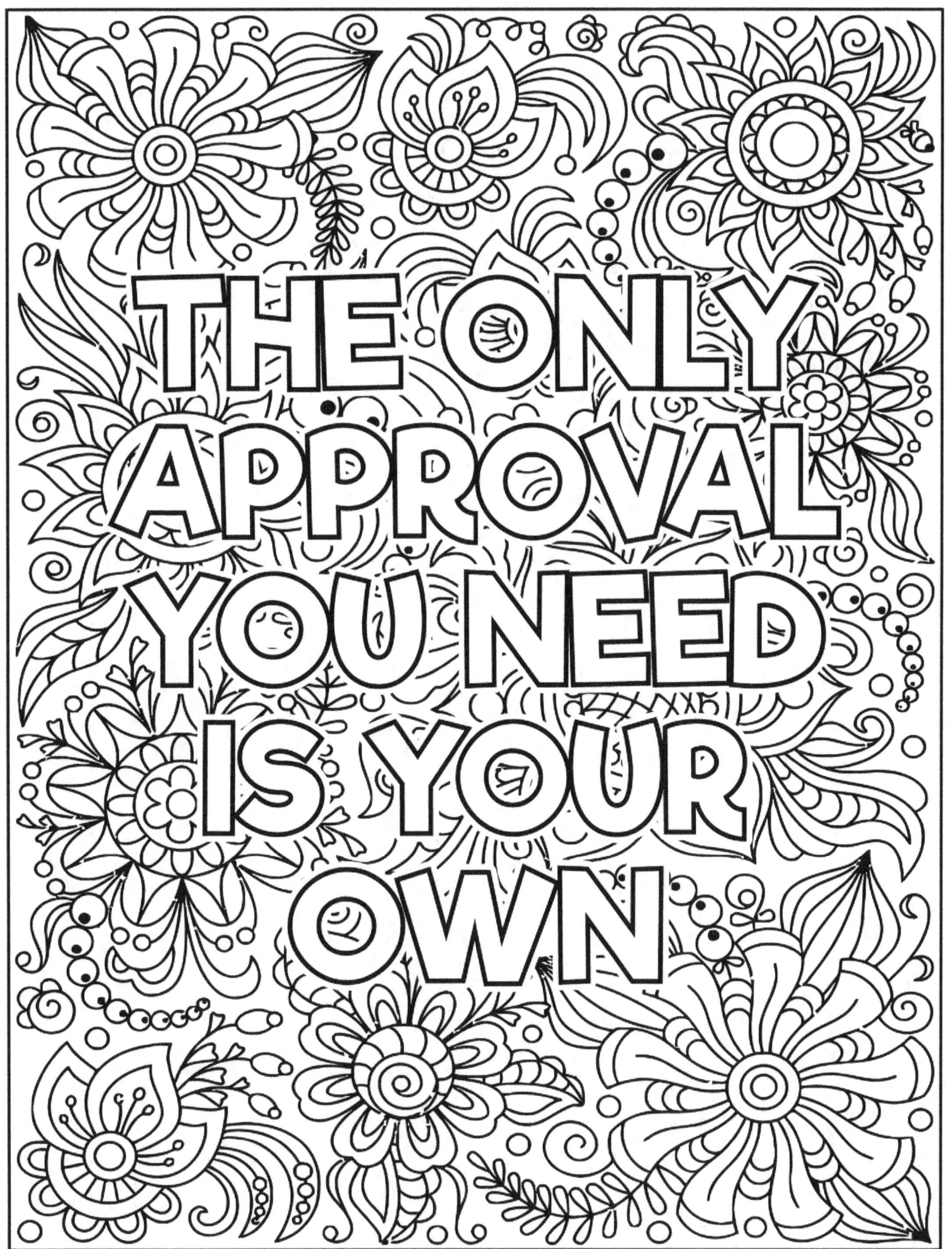

THE ONLY
APPROVAL
YOU NEED
IS YOUR
OWN

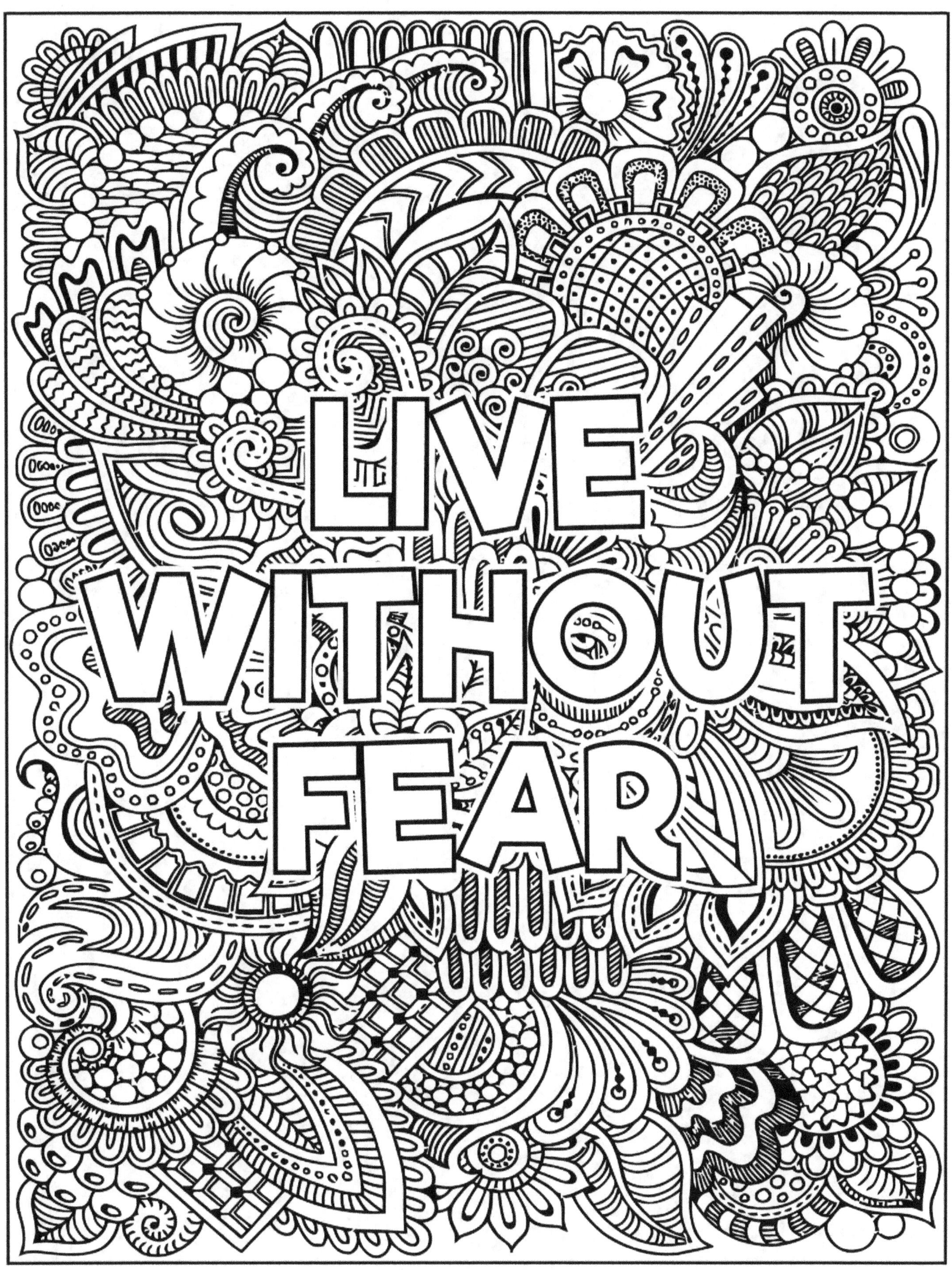

LIVE
WITHOUT
FEAR

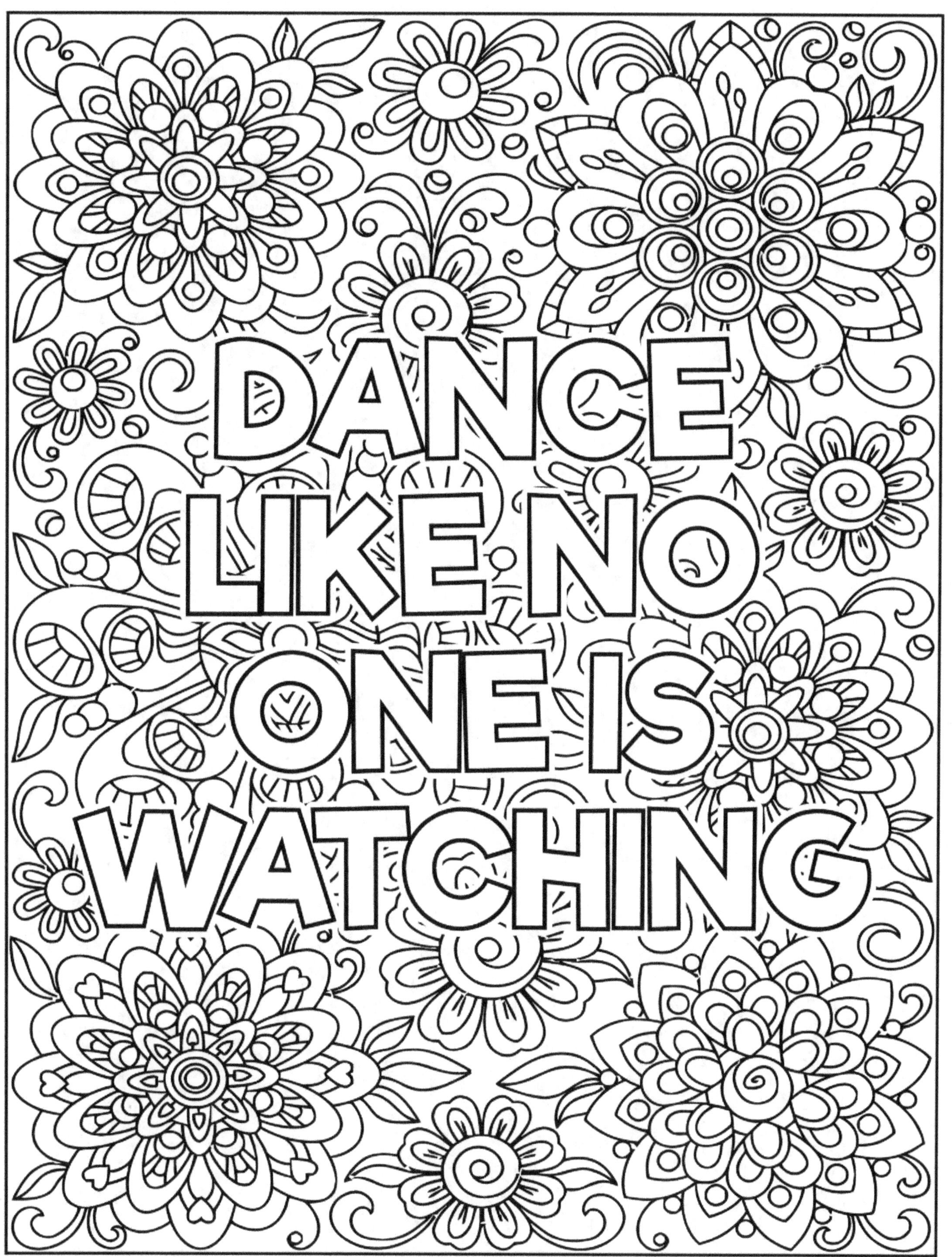

DANCE
LIKE NO
ONE IS
WATCHING

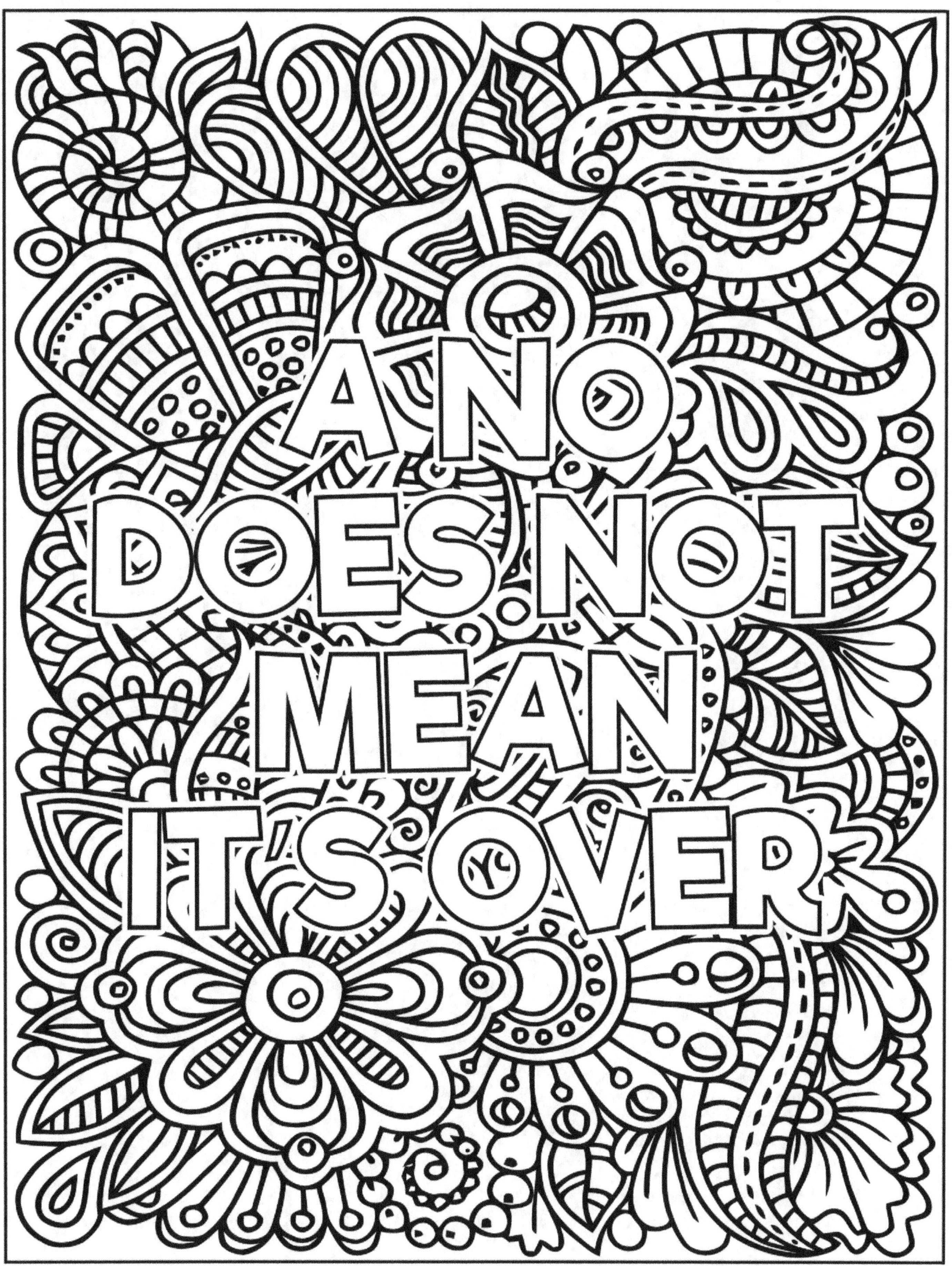
A NO
DOES NOT
MEAN
IT'S OVER

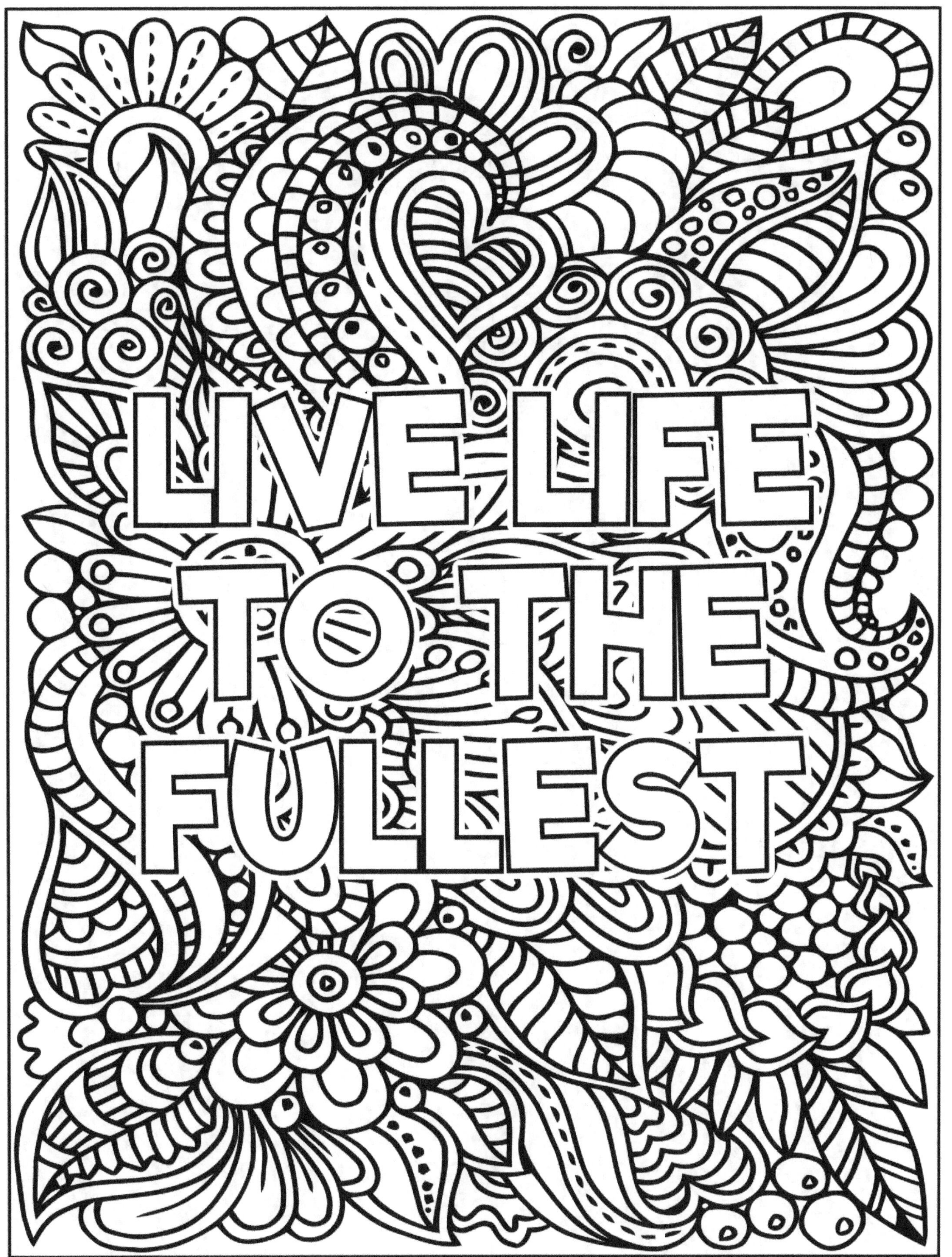

LIVE LIFE
TO THE
FULLEST

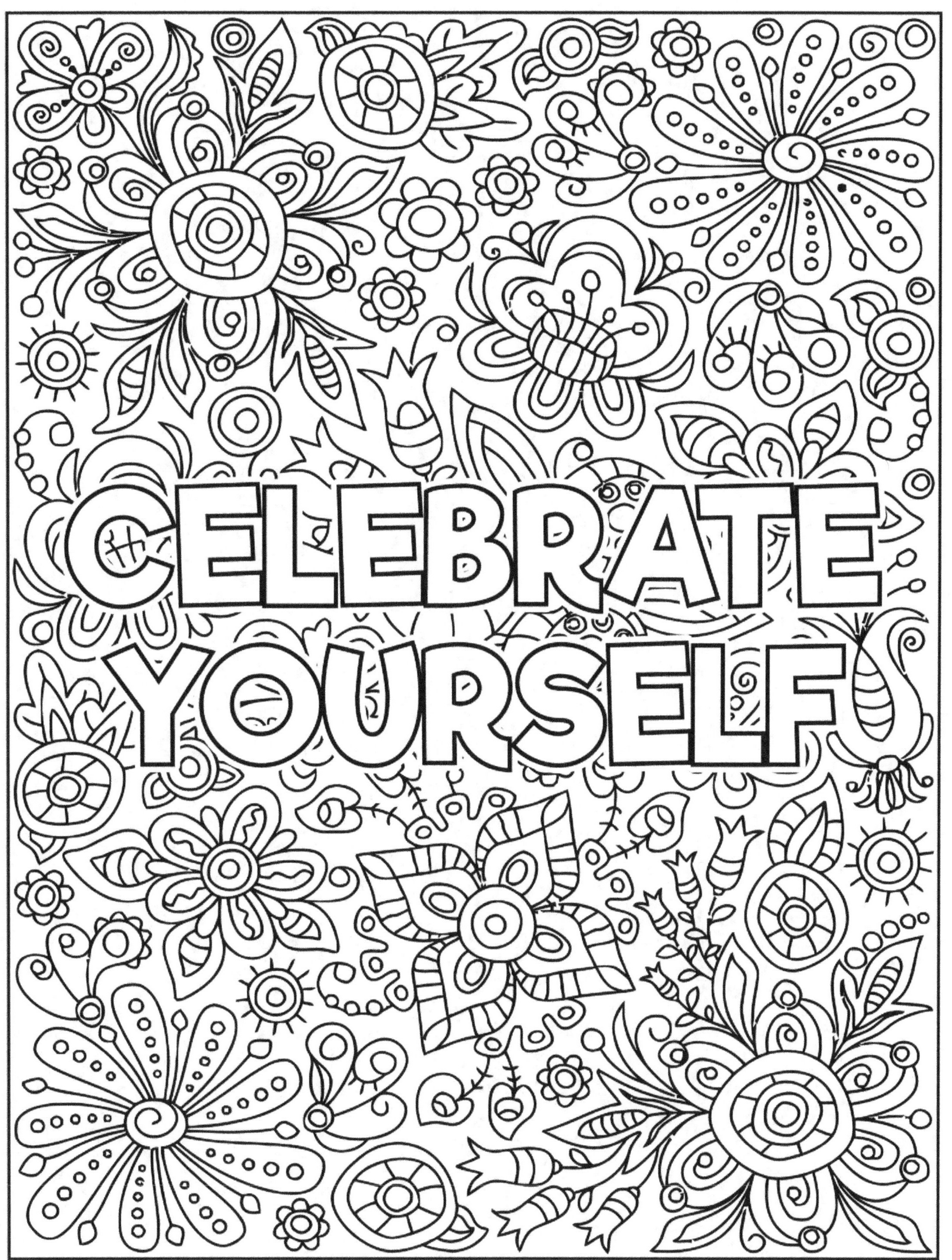

CELEBRATE
YOURSELF

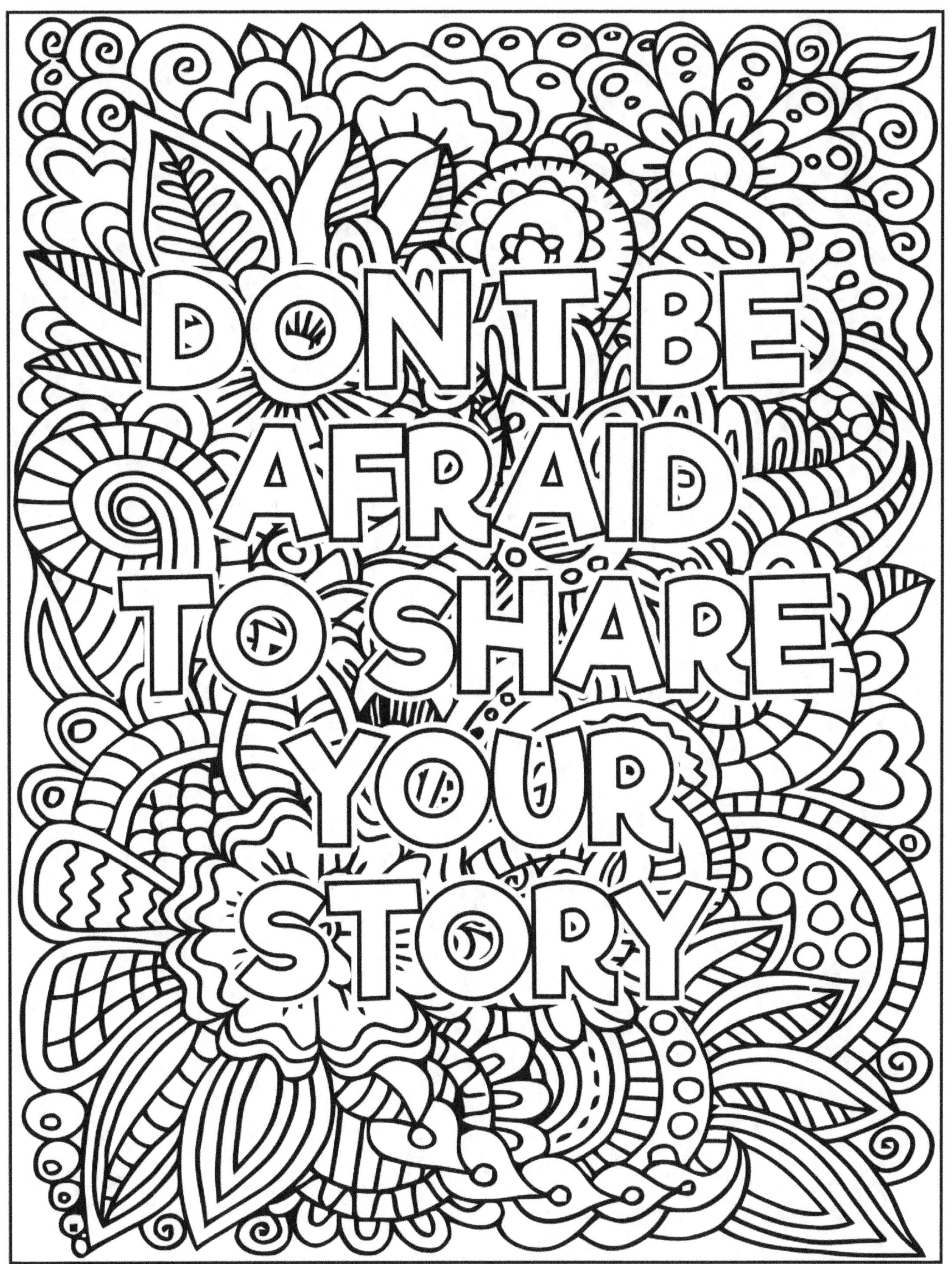

DON'T BE
AFRAID
TO SHARE
YOUR
STORY

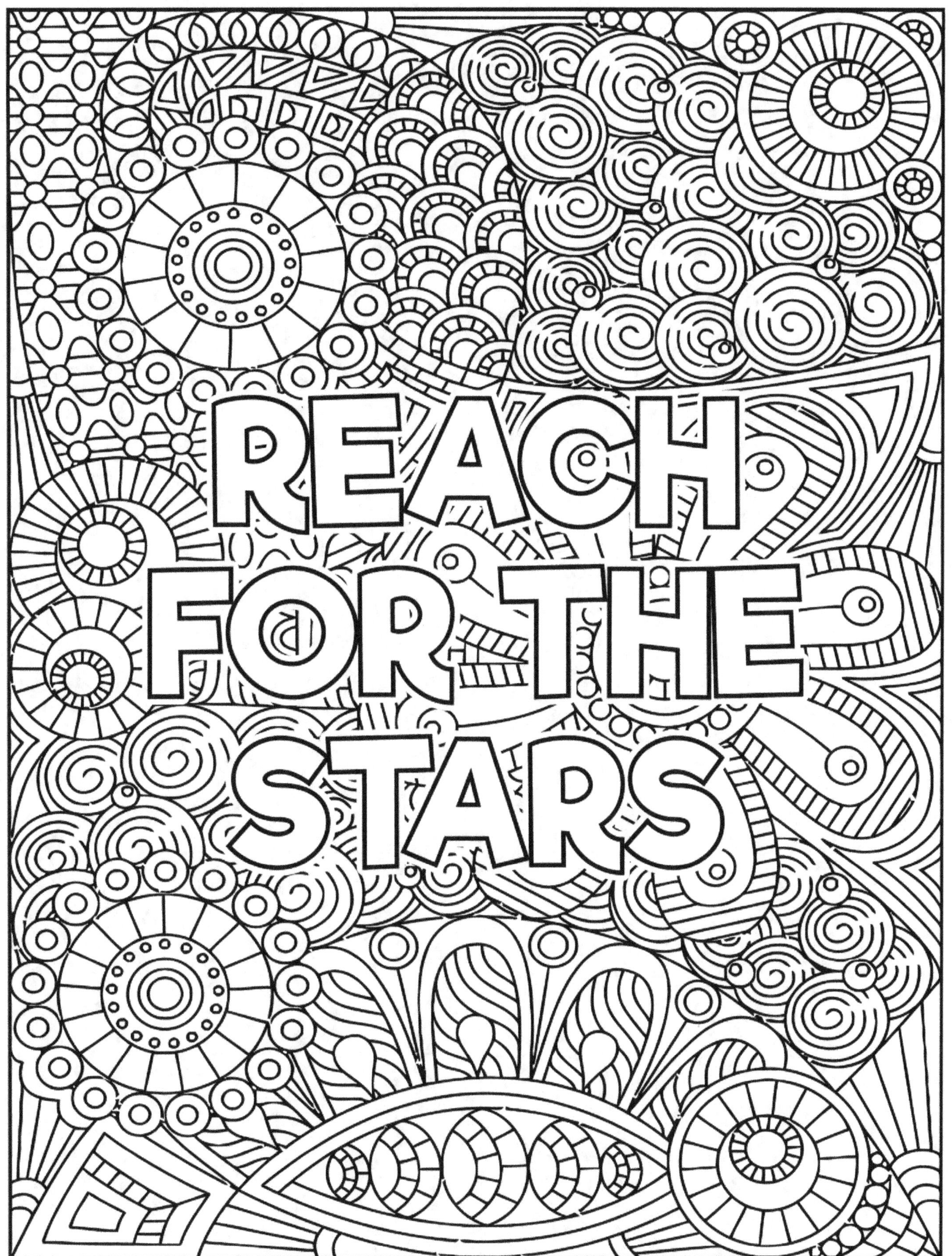

REACH
FOR THE
STARS

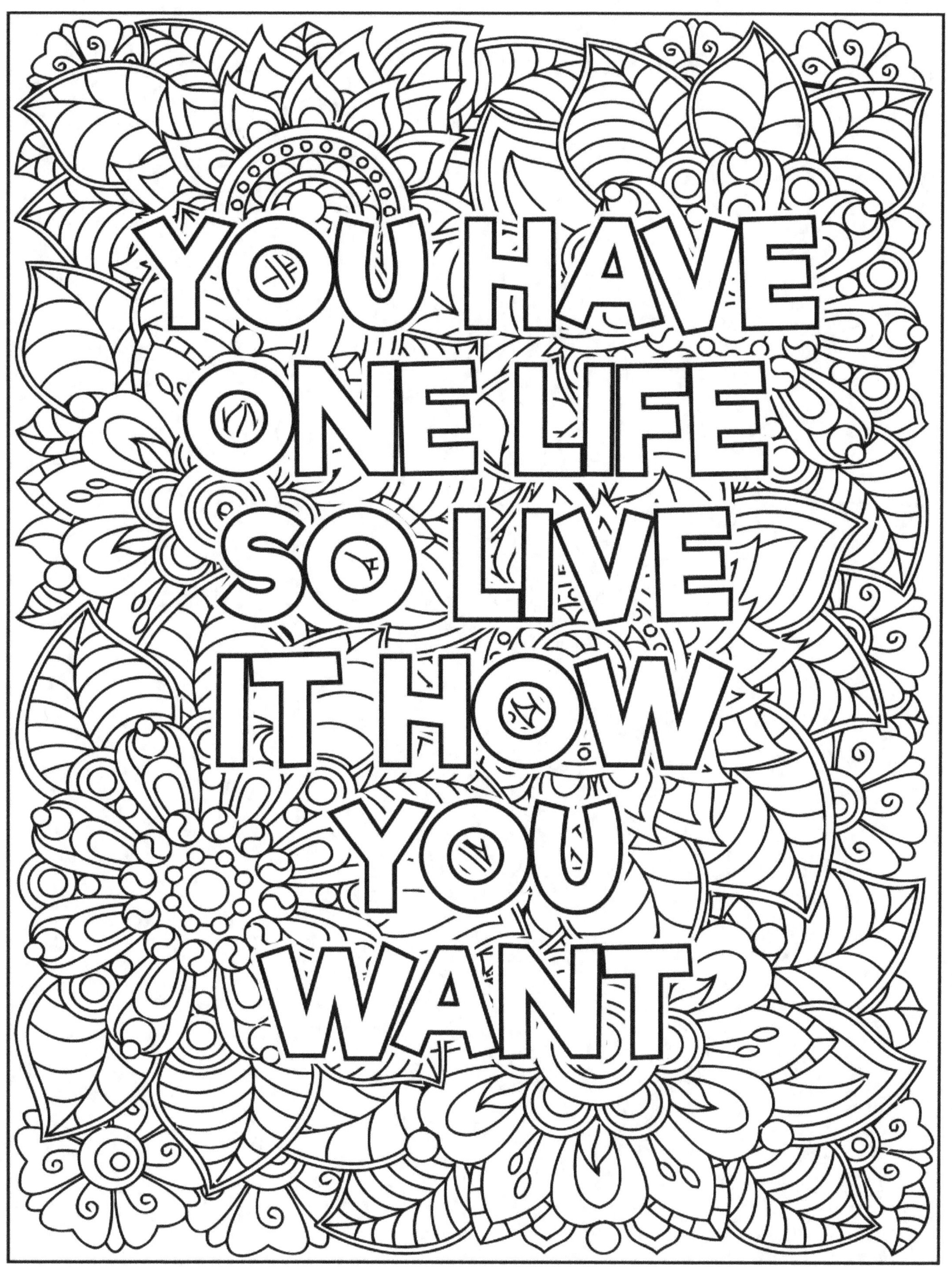

YOU HAVE
ONE LIFE
SO LIVE
IT HOW
YOU
WANT

FIND
YOUR
PURPOSE

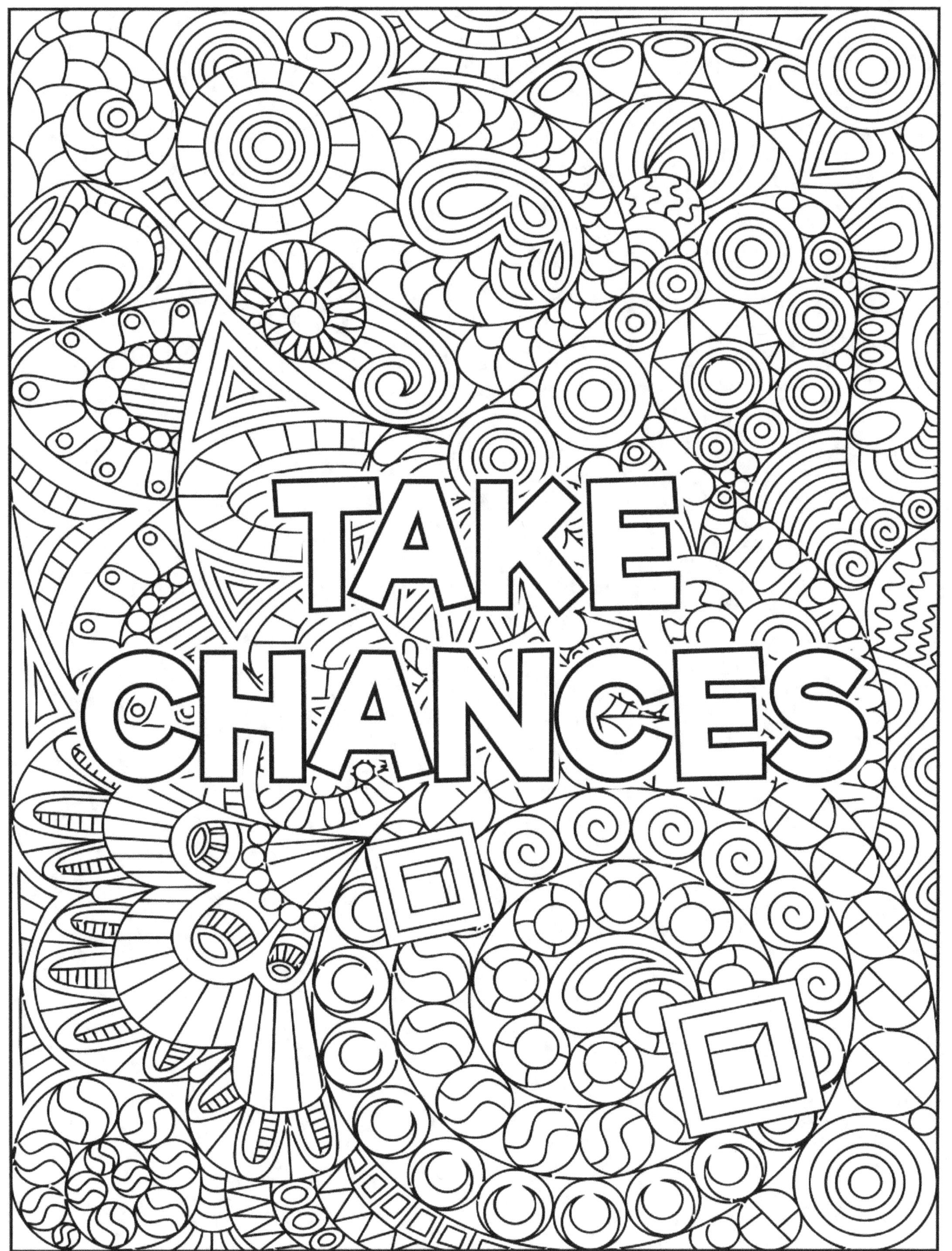
TAKE
CHANCES

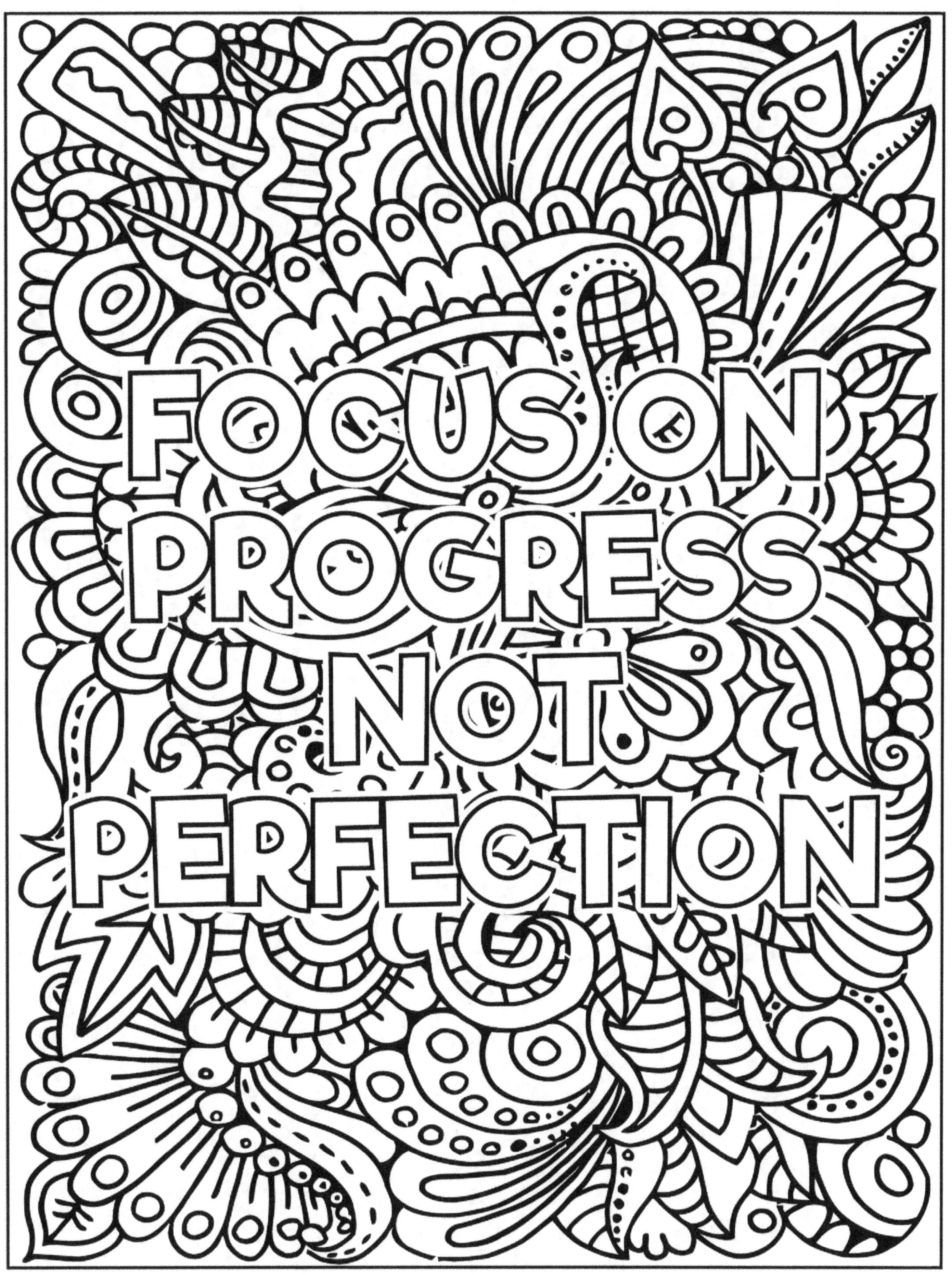
FOCUS ON
PROGRESS
NOT
PERFECTION

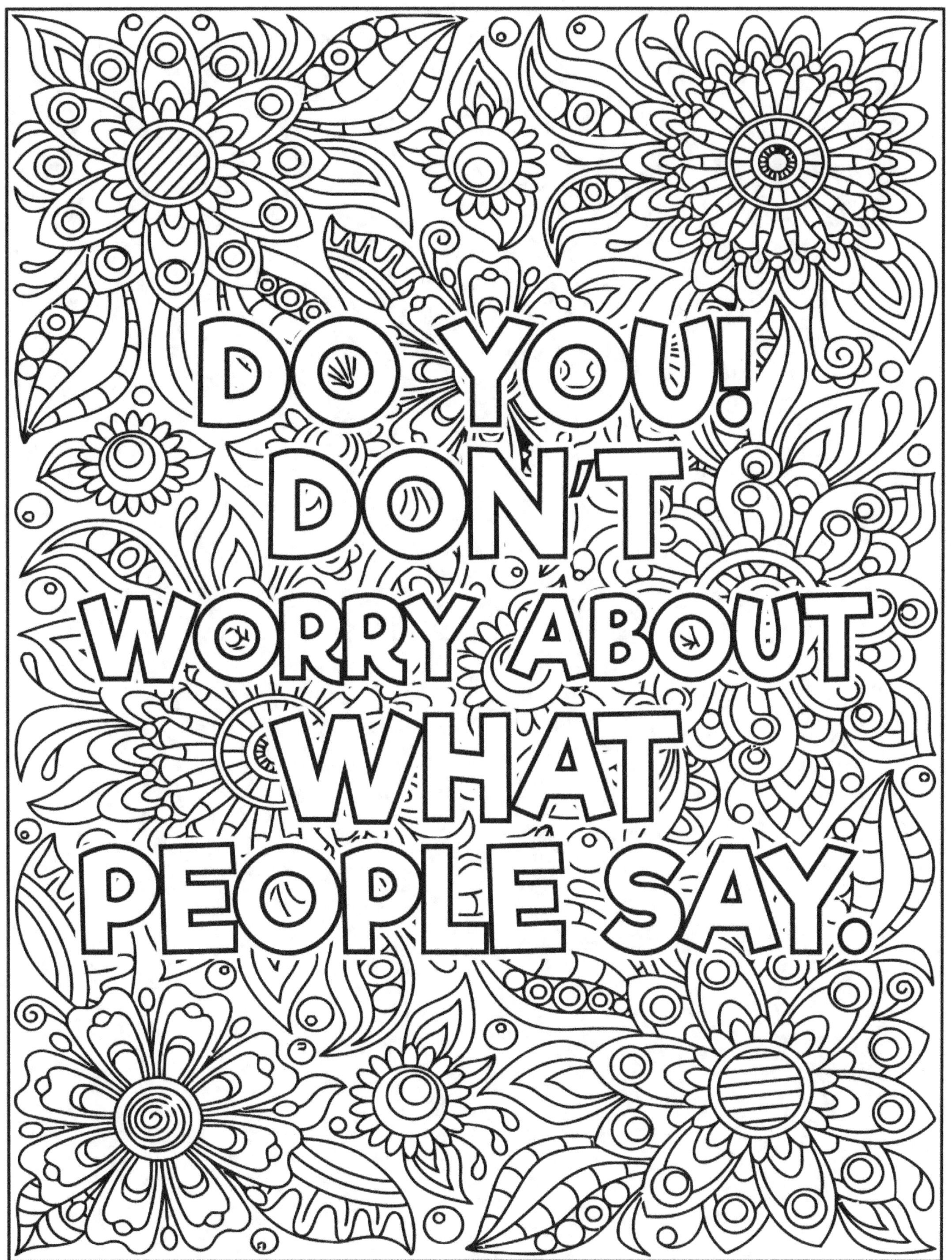

DO YOU!
DON'T
WORRY ABOUT
WHAT
PEOPLE SAY.

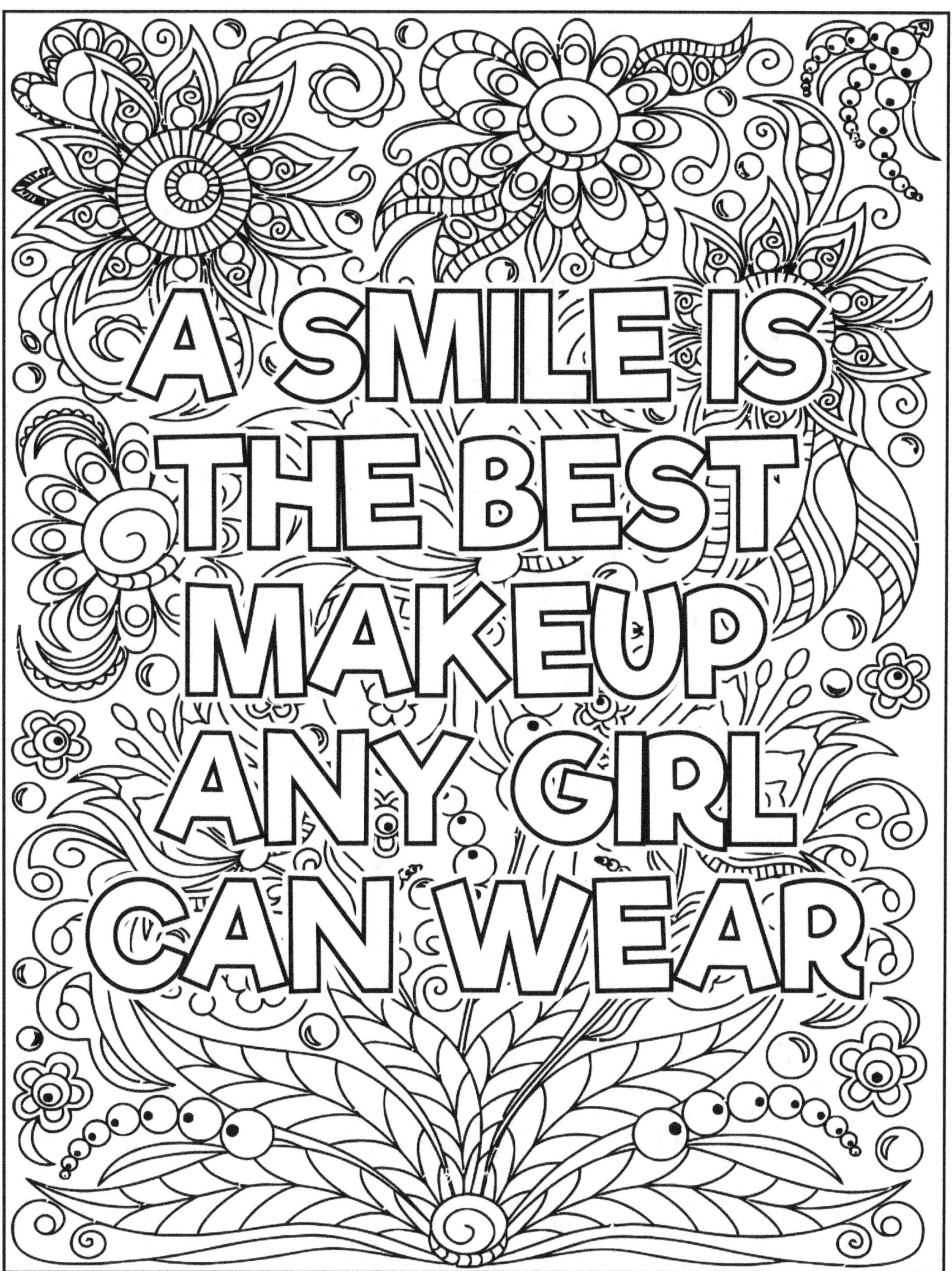

A SMILE IS
THE BEST
MAKEUP
ANY GIRL
CAN WEAR

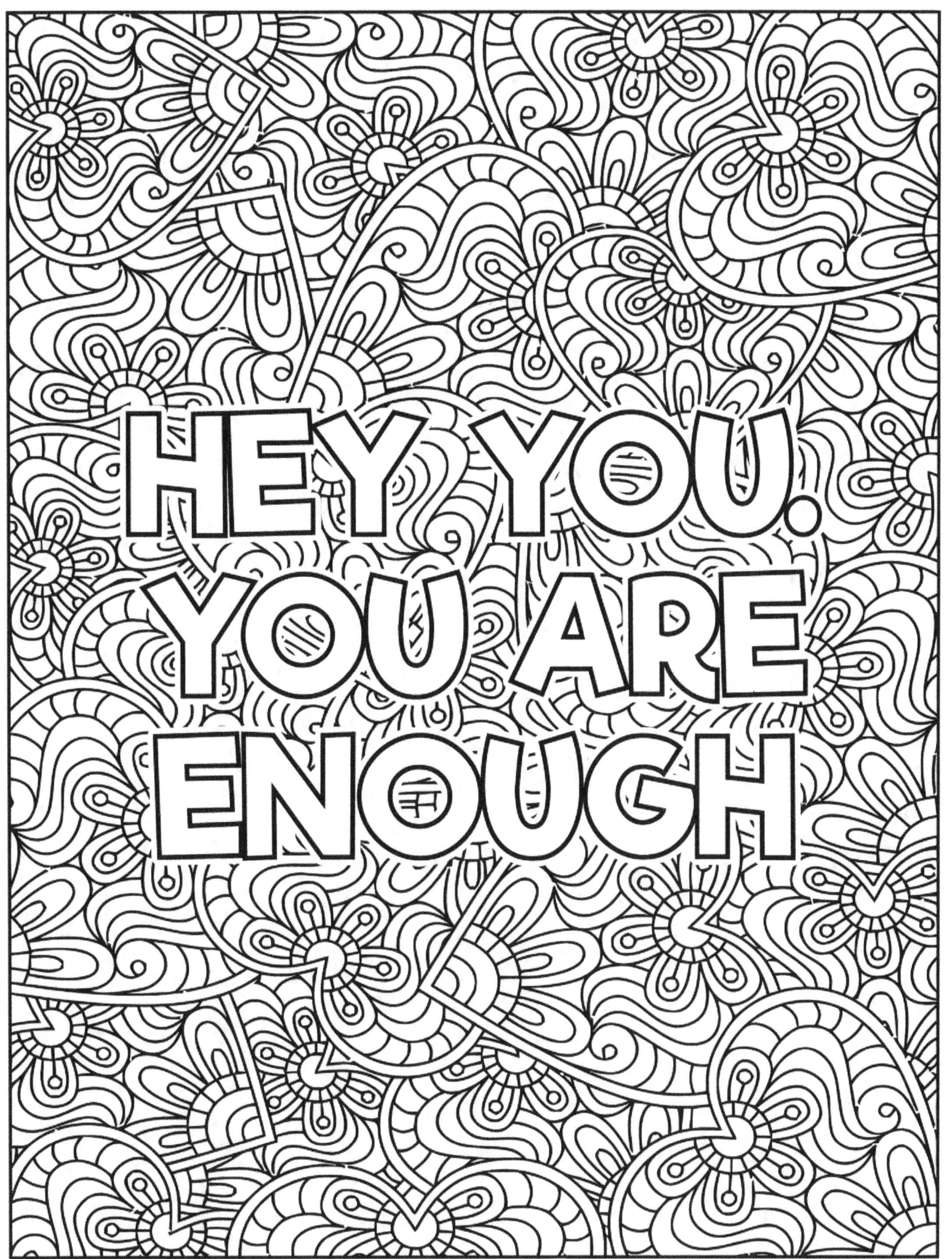

HEY YOU.
YOU ARE
ENOUGH

www.ingramcontent.com/pod-product-compliance
Lightning Source LLC
Chambersburg PA
CBHW060218120726
48004CB00008B/1866